The Quote Manual

Wisdom and Wit of the Ages

A
Fifty-year Collection
Of
Inspirational and Thought
Provoking Quotes

by

Robert G. Moscatelli

authorHOUSE™

1663 LIBERTY DRIVE, SUITE 200
BLOOMINGTON, INDIANA 47403
(800) 839-8640
WWW.AUTHORHOUSE.COM

First published by AuthorHouse 4/5/2007

ISBN: 1-4208-5331-7(sc)

Library of Congress Control Number: 2005904366

This is the **Second Editon of The Quote Manual**

Printed in the United States of America
Bloomington, Indiana

This book is printed on acid-free paper.

The quotes in this book were recorded as I heard them or encountered them in print. They are attributed herein to the speakers whom I heard say the words and to the authors to whom they were attributed when I read them. I have attempted to verify the authors of quotes attributed to specific authors and to identify the authors of quotes I encountered as "unknown," "anonymous" or where no author was indicated. Both the quotes and their authors are assumed to be accurate, although I have no way of knowing that they are with absolute confidence. In a few cases, quotes from speeches which I personally heard were recorded as accurately as possible within the limits of my memory and my ability to write quickly.

Author's Note

Chances are you have heard it said that someone "has a way with words." As a young man, I started recording the words of such people—inspirational, thought-provoking and profound things they said in a way that impressed me as worth remembering.

Most of the quotes recorded in this book resulted from my listening and reading as the years went by. I made no specific effort to cherry-pick books of quotes or proverbs. Instead, I recorded only those that surfaced in the natural course of the conduct of my life as an Army officer and a civilian and a few that I encountered in the preparation of this work.

The quotes in this anthology are not listed in any particular order or priority. Some are humorous, but most, I believe, are inspiring and worthy of serious thought.

Quotations attributed herein to a specific author were attributed to that author when I first encountered them. Quotations I attribute herein to "Anonymous" were attributed to "Anonymous" when I read or heard them. Where I indicate that the author of a quote is "Unknown," it means that I don't know who the author is. The author may be known to someone, just not to me.

I hope that the true originators of the quotes in this anthology will be flattered that I recorded their words. Obviously, I am not attempting to pass their words off as my own. This is, after all, a book of quotes. Either I failed to record their names when I encountered their words, or their names were not associated with their words when I heard or read them.

I encourage you, the reader, to have a highlighter handy the first time you read this anthology. I believe you'll find that you will spread a lot of yellow on these pages as you identify for future reference the quotes that are particularly meaningful to you.

Read, enjoy and benefit.

Bob Moscatelli
April, 2005

Table of Contents

"A short saying

oft contains much wisdom"

Sophocles

Potpourri

(These quotes don't seem to fit appropriately into any of the other subject headings in this book.)

"I expect to pass through life but once. If, therefore, there be any kindness I can show, or any good thing I can do to any fellow being, let me do it now, for I shall not pass this way again."

William Penn
English Statesman

"It has been my experience that superior people are attracted by challenge. By setting our standards low and making our life soft, we have, quite automatically and unconsciously, assured ourselves of mediocre people."

William Lederer
Eugene Burdick
The Ugly American

"One thing I have learned in my long years of public service is that whenever you are near a bathroom, use it."

Prince Philip
Great Britain

"A machine, no matter how complicated looking, is the most simple of things. A man, no matter how simple looking, is the most complicated of things."

John Masters
Author

"There are some people who use statistics as a drunkard uses a lamppost—for support rather than illumination."

Benjamin Disraeli
British Statesman, Author

"Silence is the best answer for a fool."

Nigerian Saying

"Too often we insult the young because we don't ask them for the sacrifices they are capable of."

Unknown

"Never look down on those who look up to you."

Mohammed Ali
Professional Boxer

"Conduct yourself with great discretion.
There's no second chance for a good first impression."

Romona Demery
Occupation Unknown

"The man who does not read good books has no advantage over the man who can't read them."

Mark Twain
Author

"Form good habits. They're as hard to break as bad ones."

Unknown

"You can get much farther with a kind word and a gun than you can with a kind word alone."

Al Capone
Gangster

"There is nothing more obnoxious than a braggart who can back up his claims."

Unknown

"Uncritical toleration is the most consistent mark of a decadent society."

Arnold Toynbee
British Historian

"It is not fair to ask of others what you are not willing to do yourself."

Eleanor Roosevelt
Humanitarian, Writer

"The steam from a pot of good soup is its best advertisement."

Unknown

"Gregariousness is always the refuge of mediocrity."

Boris Pasternak
<u>Dr. Zhivago</u>

"Learn to disagree without being disagreeable."

Unknown

"Always remember that you're unique, just like everyone else."

Unknown

"It is far easier to stay out of trouble than it is to get out of trouble."

Unknown

"Never get into a fight with a pig. You both get dirty and he enjoys it."

Creighton Abrams
General, Chief of Staff,
U.S. Army

"It's OK to ask dumb questions. They're easier to handle than dumb mistakes."

Unknown

"I was glad to be able to answer promptly and I did. I said I didn't know."

Mark Twain
Author

"Talk is cheap because supply exceeds demand."

Unknown

"All that is necessary for the triumph of evil is that good men do nothing."

Edmund Burke
British Statesman

"Humility is a thing that as soon as you realize you've got it, you've lost it."

Unknown

"Don't try to become well known. Try to become worth knowing."

Unknown

"No imitation was ever a masterpiece."

F. M. Slim
British General

"You can always tell a fanatic. A fanatic is a person who continues to redouble his effort long after he has forgotten his purpose."

George Santayana
Philosopher, Poet

"Men who borrow their opinions can never repay their debts."

Unknown

"Any problem thoroughly understood is fairly simple."

Charles Kettering
Engineer, Inventor

"You never go wrong doing the right thing."

Bob Moscatelli
Author, Soldier

"Where one stands depends upon where one sits."

Unknown

"The trouble with books is that one must read so many bad ones to find something really good."

Napoleon
Emperor or France

"There are no priorities among essentials."

Unknown

"Good steel comes out of a hot furnace."

Unknown

"Be true to your teeth or your teeth will be false to you."

Unknown

"Hold your friends close; hold your enemies closer."

Italian Saying

"A wise man knows everything; a shrewd one, everybody."

Unknown

"The most important thing that parents can teach their children is how to get along without them."

Frank Clark
Occupation Unknown

"In a calm sea, every man is a pilot."

John Ray
English Naturalist

"The weak can never forgive. Forgiveness is an attribute of the strong."

Mahatma Gandhi
Hindu Nationalist

"If you want to keep something concealed from your enemy, do not disclose it to your friend."

Solomon Gabriel
Occupation Unknown

"Never compete with a man who has nothing to lose."

Unknown

"The distance doesn't matter. It is only the first step that is difficult."

Marie Chamrond
Occupation Unknown

"I would rather be on the ground wishing I were in the air than in the air wishing I were on the ground."

Waiting Room Sign
Army Air Field
Heidelberg, FRG, 1971

"There is but one reason why anyone asks you to sign an agreement or any piece of paper. He thinks there might come a time when you wish you had not signed it—when you might want to deny what your signature affirms."

Eric Reisfeld
Occupation Unknown

"Prescription without diagnosis is malpractice."

Unknown

"Well-timed silence hath more eloquence than speech."

Martin Tupper
Occupation Unknown

"Be reasonable. See things my way."

Anonymous

"If you do the things you need to do when you need to do them, then someday you can do the things you want to do when you want to do them."

Zig Zigler
Motivational Speaker

"The superior man is easy to serve and difficult to please."

Confucius
Chinese Philosopher

"Speak softly. If you really want to be heard, lower your voice."

Terri Levine
Occupation Unknown

"If you want to be the top banana, you have to start at the bottom of the bunch."

Unknown

"When a man is wrapped up in himself, he makes a pretty small package."

John Ruskin
English Writer

"Remember: If all possible objections must first be overcome, nothing significant will ever get done."

Charles Kettering
Engineer, Inventor

"If you don't know jewels, know your jeweler."

Unknown

"When speaking to your children: say what you mean, mean what you say and don't be mean when you say it."

Unknown

"What gets us into trouble is not what we don't know. It's what we know for sure that just ain't so."

Yogi Berra
Baseball Player
Poor Man's Philosopher

"Anger is not a useful emotion."

Unknown

"When does life begin? When the kids leave home and the dog dies."

Unknown

"Iron rusts from disuse, stagnant water loses its purity and in cold weather becomes frozen; even so does inaction sap the vigors of the mind."

Leonardo Da Vinci
Italian Artist, Engineer

"The closest we ever come to perfection is when we write our resumes."

H. Jackson Brown
A Father's Book Of Wisdom

"People will not change until the pain of changing becomes less than the pain of staying the same."

Bob Pike
Author, Trainer

"I love to quote statistics. They can be so misleading."

Unknown

"Be nice to your kids. They choose your nursing home."

Unknown

"Too much of a good medicine can kill a patient."

Unknown

"Clear your mind of can't."

Samuel Johnson
English Author, Critic

"A wise person questions himself, the fool others."

Henri Arnold
Occupation Unknown

"A jury consists of twelve persons chosen to decide who has the better lawyer."

Robert Frost
Poet

"The enemy of my enemy is my friend."

Unknown

"Those who do not feel pain seldom think that it is felt."

Samuel Johnson
English Critic, Author

"Nothing arouses ambition so much as the trumpet clang of another's fame."

Baltasar Gracian
Occupation Unknown

"If we had no faults of our own, we would not take so much pleasure in noticing those of others."

Francois,
Duc de la Rochefoucauld

"The only way to get rid of temptation is to yield to it."

Oscar Wilde
Irish Poet, Wit

"Most people have seen worse things in private than they pretend to be shocked at in public."

Edgar Howe
Novelist, Essayist

"You raise your voice when you should reinforce your argument."

Samuel Johnson
English Critic, Author

"Those not present are always wrong."

Phillipe Destouches
Occupation Unknown

"One-half of the troubles of this life can be traced to saying 'yes' too quickly and not saying 'no' soon enough."

Josh Billings
Occupation Unknown

"Sometimes the best way to convince someone he is wrong is to let him have his way."

Red O'Donnell
Occupation Unknown

"You can never do a kindness too soon, for you never know how soon it will be too late."

Ralph Waldo Emerson
Philosopher, Poet

"A man cannot be too careful in the choice of his enemies."

Oscar Wilde
Irish Dramatist, Wit

"No one is completely worthless. He can even serve as a bad example."

Mr. Newman
Executive, General Electric Corp.

"If Columbus had an advisory committee, he would probably still be at the dock."

Arthur Goldberg
Lawyer, Jurist

"A favor well-bestowed is almost as great an honor to him who confers it as to him who receives it."

Sir Richard Steele
English Essayist

"Salud, amor y pesetas y tiempo para gozarlas."
"Health, love and money and time to enjoy them."

Mexican Toast

"The Clairvoyance Society of Greater London will not meet next Tuesday because of unforeseen circumstances."

Advertisement
"Financial Times"

"When you can't change the direction of the wind—adjust your sails."

H. Jackson Brown
A Father's Book of Wisdom

"And this, too, shall pass away."

Edward Polonius
Occupation Unknown

"The deepest principle of human nature is the craving to be appreciated."

William James
Philosopher

"No guest is so welcome in a friend's house that he will not become a nuisance after three days."

Titus Plautus
Roman Comic Playwright

"In prosperity our friends know us; in adversity we know our friends."

John Collins
Occupation Unknown

16

"Love your neighbor, yet pull not down your hedge."

George Herbert
Occupation Unknown

"Sacred cows make good hamburger."

Unknown

"We recognize that flattery is poison, but its perfume intoxicates us."

Charles Vartlet
Occupation Unknown

"All the people like us are We, and everyone else is They."

Rudyard Kipling
English Author

"When the well's dry, we know the worth of water."

Benjamin Franklin
Statesman, Scientist

"What the world needs is more geniuses with humility. There are so few of us left."

Oscar Levant
Pianist, Wit

"If it were necessary to tolerate in other people everything that one permits himself, life would be unbearable."

Georges Courteline
Occupation Unknown

"One does not wander aimlessly toward excellence."

Unknown

"Consistency is the last refuge of the unimaginative."

Oscar Wilde
Irish Poet, Wit

"Conceit is a weird disease. It makes everybody sick except the one who's got it."

Unknown

"When science discovers the center of the universe, a lot of people will be disappointed to find they are not it."

Bernard Baily
Occupation Unknown

"If I've told you once, I've told you a million times. Don't exaggerate!"

Unknown

"A mind is like a parachute. It only works when it's open."

Unknown

"It is better to be hated for what you are than to be loved for what you are not."

Andre Gide
French Writer

"Television is an invention that permits you to be entertained in your living room by people you wouldn't have in your home."

David Frost
Television Personality

"I have the strength of ten......because my heart is pure."

Unknown

"Some people are making such thorough plans for rainy days that they aren't enjoying today's sunshine."

William Feather
Naturalist, Photographer

"The things that will destroy us are: politics without principle; pleasure without conscience; wealth without work; knowledge without character; business without morality; science without humanity; and worship without sacrifice."

Mahatma Gandhi
Hindu Nationalist

"There are those, I know, who will reply that the liberation of humanity, the freedom of man and mind, is nothing but a dream. They are right. It is. It is the American Dream."

Archibald Macleish
Poet

"It is better to deserve honors and not have them than to have them and not deserve them."

Mark Twain
Author

"When women are depressed, they either eat or go shopping. Men invade another country."

Elayne Boosler
Comedian

"Insanity is hereditary; you can get it from your children."

Sam Levenson
Author, Humorist

"Everyone who got where he is had to start where he was."

Robert Louis Stevenson
Scottish Poet, Novelist

"If you find yourself in a hole, stop digging."

Will Rogers
Humorist, Author

"Of all sad words of tongue or pen, the saddest are these: 'It might have been.'"

John Greenleaf Whittier
Poet, Author

"A promiscuous person is someone who is getting more sex than you are."

Victor Lownes
Author

"I like children, if they're properly cooked."

W. C. Fields
Comedian

"Forgive and forget. Sour grapes make for a lousy wine."

H. Jackson Brown
A Father's Book of Wisdom

"When it comes to life, live like there is no tomorrow. Love like you won't get hurt, work like you don't need the money and dance like no one is watching."

Unknown

"You are fulfilled not by what you take but by what you give."

Madellin Manning-Mims
Occupation Unknown

"The world is a book, and the person who stays home reads but one page."

William Shakespeare
English Playwright

"You don't have to brush all your teeth.....just the ones you want to keep."

Sign In Dentist's Office

"If you think nobody cares if you're alive, try missing a couple of car payments."

Earl Wilson
Journalist

"Be studious in your profession, and you will be learned. Be industrious and frugal and you will be rich. Be sober and temperate, and you will be healthy. Be in general virtuous, and you will be happy. At least, you will, by such conduct, stand the best chance for such consequences."

Benjamin Franklin
Statesman, Author
Letter to John Alleyn

"Whatever is worth doing is worth doing well."

Lord Chesterfield
English Statesman, Author

"One of the annoying things about believing in free will and individual responsibility is the difficulty of finding someone to blame your problems on. And when you do find somebody, it's remarkable how often his picture turns up on your driver's license."

P. J. O'Rourke
Political Humorist

"Never say all you know, but always know all you say."

Unknown

"If you wish others to keep your secret, first, keep it yourself."

Unknown

"Criticism from a friend is better than flattery from an enemy."

Unknown

"The best time for you to hold your tongue is the time you feel you must say something or bust."

Josh Billings
Author, Humorist

"Some guy hit my fender the other day, and I said unto him, 'Be fruitful and multiply.' But not in those exact words......."

Woody Allen
Actor, Commedian

23

"The farther backwards you can look, the farther forward you are likely to see."

Winston Churchill
British Prime Minister

"Bootlickers are even more obvious to your superiors than they are to you. Don't compete with them."

Colin Powell
Assistant Division Commander
4th Infantry Division, 1982

"Always keep your words soft and sweet, just in case you have to eat them."

Unknown

"Beware of inspirations that take wing on the vapors of your second martini."

Eno Putain
Occupation Unknown

<u>Attitude</u>

"No one can make you feel inferior without your consent."

Eleanor Roosevelt
Humanitarian, Diplomat

"Live! Life is a banquet, and most of you poor sons-of-bitches are starving to death!"

From The Play "Auntie Mame"

"Whether you think you can or you can't, you are right."

Henry Ford
Industrialist

"If you don't stand for something, you'll fall for anything."

Unknown

"There is no hope for a satisfied man."

Frederick Bonfils
Founder, "The Denver Post"

"Feed your faith and doubt will starve."

Unknown

"Pray as if it were up to God; work as if it were up to you."

Unknown

"A positive attitude may not solve all your problems, but it will annoy enough people to make it worth the effort."

Herm Albright
Occupation Unknown

"When contentment sets in, progress stops."

Unknown

"A great man shows his greatness by the way he treats little men."

Thomas Carlyle
English Essayist, Historian

"The way I see it, if you want the rainbow, you gotta put up with the rain."

Dolly Parton
Singer, Song Writer

"Nothing in the world can take the place of persistence. Talent will not; nothing is more common than unsuccessful men with talent. Genius will not; unrewarded genius is almost a proverb. Education will not; the world is full of educated derelicts. Persistence and determination alone are omnipotent."

Calvin Coolidge
Politician, U.S. President

"Most people are about as happy as they make up their minds to be."

Abraham Lincoln
U. S. President

"Challenges can be stepping stones or stumbling blocks. It's a matter of how you view them."

Unknown

"The starting point of all achievement is desire. Keep this constantly in mind. Weak desires bring weak results, just as a small amount of fire makes a small amount of heat."

Napoleon Hill
Author, Motivational Speaker

"The man who really wants to do something finds a way; the man who doesn't finds an excuse."

Unknown

"What matters is not the size of the dog in the fight, but the size of the fight in the dog."

Bear Bryant
Football Coach, Alabama

"I found that I could find the energy….that I could find the determination to keep on going. I learned that your mind can amaze your body, if you just keep telling yourself, I can do it….I can do it….I can do it."

Jon Erickson
Author

<u>Business</u>

"Good people are tough to get, tough to manage, and tough to hang on to. They make you run harder and faster. They push you, they make you stretch. They keep you on your toes. In short, aside from their contribution to the corporate effort, they're the best thing in the world for you."

Louis Lundborg
Chairman, Bank of America

"A lawyer with a briefcase can steal more than a thousand men with guns."

Mario Puzo
Author

"The camel is the result of a committee which was formed to design a horse."

Hyman Rickover
Admiral, U. S. Navy

"Never tell people how to do things. Tell them what to do, and they will surprise you with their ingenuity."

George S. Patton
General, U. S. Army

"When you dance with a customer, let him lead."

H. Jackson Brown
<u>A Father's Book of Wisdom</u>

"It's lonely at the top, but you eat better."

Unknown

"I want you to speak freely just like the other guy that used to work here."

Mr. Newman
Director, Engines Group
General Electric Corp.
U. S. Army War College
8 Dec 77

"If you aren't talking to your clients, somebody else is."

Unknown

"Successful salesman: someone who has found a cure for the common cold shoulder."

Robert Orben
Occupation Unknown

"Characteristics that top executives must have for success:

    They must be courteous.

    They must credit others for accomplishments.

    They must be truthful.

    They must be concise in speaking and writing.

    They must be generous."

Unknown

"The kind of people I look for to fill top management spots are the eager beavers, the mavericks. These are the guys who try to do more than they're expected to do—they always reach."

Lee Iacocca
CEO, Chrysler Corporation

"All successful employers are stalking men who will do the unusual, men who think, men who attract attention by performing more than is expected of them."

Charles Schwab
Discount Broker

"One of the most insistent things in life is that you are ultimately judged by what you actually accomplish. The busy world of workers gives scant attention to assertion, explanation, protest, apology or complaint. What counts most is not promise, but performance. Good work speaks for itself, therefore achieve something first, and talk about it afterward if you must. Time spent in promises, regrets, and professions, is usually unavailing. The way to do things is not to dream about them nor wish for them, but to do them. The distinguished men in all times have been prodigious workers, earnestly intent upon securing actual results. The present age is intensely practical, and more than ever the race is to the alert, the energetic and the industrious."

Grenville Kleiser
Author

"Always remember, you have to get along with your boss. Your boss doesn't have to get along with you."

Unknown

"Inequality of knowledge is the key to a sale."

Deil O. Gustafson
Occupation Unknown

"The best executive is the one who has sense enough to pick good men to do what he wants done and the self-restraint to keep from meddling with them while they do it."

Theodore Roosevelt
U. S. President

<u>Courage</u>

"It is curious that physical courage should be so common in the world and moral courage so rare."

Mark Twain
Author

"Prefiero morir de pie que vivir de rodillas."

"I prefer to die on my feet than to live on my knees."

Emiliano Zapata
Mexican Revolutionist

"The world belongs to the meat eaters."

Unknown

"Some have been thought brave because they were afraid to run away."

Thomas Fuller
Occupation Unknown

"Nobody cares if you can't dance well. Just get up and dance."

Unknown

"Few men are born brave. Many become so through training and force of discipline."

Flavius Vegetius Renatus
Roman Writer

"It is out of the impact of ideals mainly that men develop the strength to face situations from which it would be normal to run away."

The Armed Forces Officer

"Never let the fear of striking out get in your way."

Babe Ruth
Baseball Player

Definitions

"A committee is a cul-de-sac down which ideas are lured and then quietly strangled."

Barnett Cocks
Author

"A liberal is a man who will give away everything he doesn't own."

Frank Dane
Author

"Tact is the knack of making a point without making an enemy."

Sir Isaac Newton
English Scientist

"Conscience is the inner voice that warns us somebody may be looking."

H. L. Mencken
Satirist, Social Critic

"A banker is someone who lends you an umbrella when the sun is shining, and who asks for it back when it starts to rain."

Unknown

"Filing cabinet: A place to lose things alphabetically."

Unknown

"A flatterer is a man who tells you your opinion and not his own."

Anonymous

"Social tact is making your company feel at home, even though you wish they were."

Anonymous

"A diplomatist is a man who always remembers a woman's birthday but never remembers her age."

Robert Frost
Poet

"A bank is a place that will lend you money if you can prove that you don't need it."

Bob Hope
Comedian

"An idealist is one who, on realizing that a rose smells better than a cabbage, concludes that it will also make better soup."

H. L. Mencken
Satirist, Social Critic

"Bore: A person who talks when you wish him to listen."

Ambrose Bierce
Author

"Faith may be defined briefly as the illogical belief in the occurrence of the improbable."

H. L. Mencken
Satirist, Social Critic

"A team effort is a lot of people doing what I say."

Michael Winner
British Film Director

"The taxpayer: That's someone who works for the federal government but doesn't have to take the civil service examination."

Ronald Reagan
U. S. President

"Duty: Doing what should be done, when it should be done, without being asked or ordered to do it."

U. S. Army Definition

"Acquaintance: A person whom we know well enough to borrow money from, but not well enough to lend money to."

Unknown

"An appeaser is one who feeds a crocodile, hoping that it will eat him last."

Winston Churchill
British Statesman

"Fear is that little darkroom where negatives are developed."

"A friend is one who knows you as you are, understands where you've been, accepts who you've become and still invites you to grow."

__Education__

"If a man empties his purse into his head, no one can take it away from him. An investment in knowledge always pays the best interest."

Benjamin Franklin
Statesman, Author, Scientist

"If you think education is expensive, try ignorance."

Unknown

"It is impossible to give a soldier a good education without making him a deserter."

Henry David Thoreau
Essayist, Poet

"If the learner has failed to learn, then the teacher has failed to teach."

Unknown

"Genius is one percent inspiration and ninety-nine percent perspiration."

Thomas Edison
Inventor

"Don't limit a child to your own learning, for he was born in another time."

Anonymous

"You pay for education once. You pay for the lack of education all your life."

Unknown

"If you work on your job, you make a living; if you work on yourself, you make a fortune."

Jim Rohn
Motivational Speaker

"Live as if you were to die tomorrow. Learn as if you were to live forever."

Mahatma Gandhi
Hindu Nationalist

"America believes in education: the average college professor earns more in a year than a professional athlete earns in a whole week."

Evan Esar
Occupation Unknown

"I never learned anything while talking, but I have learned a lot while listening."

Unknown

"There's no education in the second kick of a mule."

Sam Rayburn
Speaker of the House of Representatives

"When I was a boy of fourteen, my father was so ignorant I could hardly stand to have the old man around. But when I got to be twenty-one, I was astonished at how much he had learned in seven years."

Mark Twain
Author

<u>Experience</u>

"There is no experience better for the heart than reaching down and lifting people up."

John Andrew Holmer
Occupation Unknown

"Experience keeps a dear school, but fools will learn in no other."

Benjamin Franklin
Statesman, Scientist

"The trouble with using experience as a guide is that the final exam often comes first and then the lesson."

Vernon Sanders Law
Poet
"How To Be A Winner"

"Learn from the mistakes of others. You won't live long enough to make all of them yourself."

Jane Bryant Quinn
Financial Columnist

"He who ignores history is condemned to relive it."

George Santayana
Philosopher, Poet

"There is only one thing more painful than learning from experience, and that is not learning from experience."

Archibald McLeish
Poet

"Experience is the name everyone gives to his mistakes."

Oscar Wilde
Irish Poet, Dramatist

"If you always do what you always did, you'll always get what you always got."

Unknown

Fishing/Hunting

"Virgencita, haceme pescar un pez bien grande haci no tengo que mentir."

"Little Virgin, let me catch a fish so big that I do not have to lie."

Argentinian Angler's Prayer

"The gods do not subtract from the allocated span of men's lives the hours spent in fishing."

Assyrian Saying

"Work is for people who have never learned to fish."

Unknown

"The fishing rod: A stick with a hook at one end and a fool at the other."

Samuel Johnson
English Author, Critic

"A miserable day fishing beats a great day at the office."

Unknown

"I once gave up fishing. It was the most miserable weekend of my life."

Unknown

"Fishing was invented to give otherwise upright people an acceptable outlet for lying."

Reverend George Hall

"The woods are always empty if you're a lousy hunter."

Unknown

"Fly fishing is not a matter of life and death. It's much more important than that."

Unknown

"A happy fisherman is the richest of men."

Anonymous

"There's no need to drive fifty miles to go fishing when you can depend on being just as unsuccessful near home."

Mark Twain
(Paraphrase)

"A wife and a steady job have ruined many a good hunter."

Unknown

"Man cannot fly fish and worry at the same time."

Unknown

"After eating an entire bull, a mountain lion felt so good, he started roaring. He kept it up until a hunter came along and shot him. The moral: When you're full of bull, keep your mouth shut."

Will Rogers
Humorist, Writer

"Behold the hunter. He riseth early in the morning and disturbeth the whole household. Mighty are his preparations. He goeth forth full of hope and when the day is spent, he returneth home smelling of strong drink and the truth is not in him."

Unknown

<u>Goals</u>

"The indispensable first step to getting the things you want out of life is this: decide what you want."

Ben Stein
Humorist, Political Commentator

"Obstacles are those frightful things you see when you take your eyes off your goals."

Henry Ford
Industrialist

"Better to aim high and come up short than to aim low and hit your mark."

Unknown

"Any road is the right road if you don't know where you're going."

Unknown

Great Philosophers

"Oftimes men in the game are blind to what the lookers-on see clearly."

Confucius
China

"If a man knows not what harbor he seeks, any wind is the right wind."

Seneca
Roman Empire

"Choose a job you love and you will never have to work a day in your life."

Confucius
China

"The best place to find helping hands is at the end of your own arms."

Confucius
China

"Waste not fresh tears over old griefs."

Euripides
Greece

"Our greatest glory is not in never falling, but in rising every time we fall."

Confucius
China

"Anyone can hold the helm when the sea is calm."

Publilius Syrus
Roman Empire

"When prosperity comes, don't use all of it."

Confucius
China

"What you cannot enforce, do not command."

Sophocles
Greece

"Nothing that is, needs to be, just because it was."

Hericicus
Unknown Origin

"I often regret that I have spoken; never that I have been silent."

Publilius Syrus
Roman Empire

"One must wait until the evening to know how truly splendid the day has been."

Sophocles
Greece

<u>Indecision</u>

"Who reflects too much will accomplish little."

Johann von Schiller
German Essayist

"The man who insists upon seeing with perfect clearness before he decides, never decides."

Henri-Frederic Amiel
Swiss Critic

"Too much analysis results in paralysis."

Unknown

<u>Insurance</u>

"Insurance is a little like religion. You have to get it when you don't want it in order to have it when you need it."

Unknown

"Insurance—an ingenious modern game of chance in which the player is permitted to enjoy the comfortable conviction that he is beating the man who keeps the table."

Ambrose Bierce
Author

"Insurance: In the big print, they give you coverage. In the small print, they take it away."

Unknown

"On no subject has ignorance so generally prevailed as in life insurance."

Burton Hendrick
Historian

"Of all the perils of life that threaten your life and possessions, probably none is more constant nor greater than the chance of having an accident with your car."

Nancy Golonka
<u>How To Protect What's Yours</u>

<u>Integrity/Trust</u>

"Few things help an individual more than to place responsibility upon him and to let him know that you trust him."

Booker T. Washington
Educator

"What upsets me is not that you lied to me, but that from now on I can no longer believe you."

Fredrich Nietzsche
German Philosopher, Critic

"Letting someone believe something that is not the truth is just as bad as a lie."

Movie "Maid in Manhattan"

"The imperative of ethics is integrity."

LTC Flynn
Instructor
U. S. Air Force Academy

"When faith is gone, when honor dies, the man is dead."

John Greenleaf Whittier
Poet, Author

"When my love tells me she is made of truth, I do believe her, though I know she lies."

William Shakespeare
English Playwright

"A truth that's told with bad intent beats all the lies you can invent."

William Blake
English Poet, Engraver

"Oh, what a tangled web we weave when first we practice to deceive."

Sir Walter Scott
Scottish Poet

"Many a truth is spoke in jest."

Anonymous

"Never trust a man who says 'trust me.'"

Unknown

"The best way to keep one's word is not to give it."

Napoleon
Emperor of France

"The louder he talked on his honor, the faster we counted our spoons."

Ralph Waldo Emerson
Philosopher, Poet

"We are inclined to believe those whom we do not know because they have never deceived us."

Samuel Johnson
English Critic, Author

"It is hard to tell that a man is telling the truth when you know that you would lie if you were in his place."

H. L. Mencken
Satirist, Social Critic

"No legacy is so rich as honesty."

William Shakespeare
English Playwright

"When you tell the truth, you never need to worry about your lousy memory."

H. Jackson Brown
A Father's Book of Wisdom

"A lie can travel halfway around the world while the truth is putting on its shoes."

Mark Twain
Author

"Trust in Allah, but tie your camel."

Arab Saying

"As scarce as truth is, the supply has always been in excess of the demand."

Josh Billings
Author, Humorist

"Truth is often painful to speak but soothing to live."

Unknown

"There are three kinds of lies—lies, damn lies and statistics."

Benjamin Disraeli
British Statesman, Author

"People never lie so much as after a hunt, during a war or before an election."

Otto Von Bismarck
German Statesman

"The income tax has made more liars out of the American people than golf has."

Will Rogers
Humorist, Author, Actor

"What is left when honor is lost?"

Publilius Syrus
Roman Philosopher

"This is the punishment of a liar. He is not believed even when he tells the truth."

Unknown

"If any man seeks greatness, let him forget greatness and ask for truth and he will find both."

Horace Mann
Educator

Leadership

"Watch me and do as I do."

U. S. Army Leadership Principle

"When an actor is bad, applause makes him worse."

Jules Renard
Author, Trainer

"The way to develop the best that is in a man is by appreciation and encouragement."

Charles Schwab
Discount Broker

"Getting praise is like getting paid."

Unknown

"Correction does much, but encouragement does more. Encouragement after censure is as the sun after a shower."

Johann Goethe
German Dramatist, Poet

"The creative leader recognizes talent; the successful leader harnesses talent; the wise leader rewards talent."

Unknown

"Not the cry but the flight of the wild duck leads the flock to follow."

Chinese Proverb

"The business of a leader is to turn weakness into strength, obstacles into stepping stones and disaster into triumph."

Unknown

"Leadership is the art of getting someone else to do what you want done because he wants to do it."

Dwight D. Eisenhower
U.S. President

"Think like a man of action. Act like a man of thought."

Henri Bergson
Author

"Controlling Operations

Do	Don't
Delegate Responsibility	Pass the buck
Grant necessary authority	Try to do it all yourself
Carefully consider reports received	Interfere with subordinates
Make decisions and act promptly	Fail to help subordinates in need of assistance"

"The Driver vs The Leader

The Driver	The Leader
Says "I"	Says "we"
Depends on authority	Depends on good morale
Inspires fear	Inspires enthusiasm
Throws his weight around	Throws his weight behind the task
Fixes blame for the breakdown	Fixes the breakdown
Rubs a mistake in	Rubs a mistake out
Knows how it's done	Shows how it's done
Makes work drudgery"	Makes work interesting

Author Unknown

A
Short Course
in Human Relations

"The six most important words:

I admit I made a mistake.

The five most important words:

You did a good job.

The four most important words:

What is your opinion?

The three most important words:

May I help?

The two most important words:

Thank you.

The one most important word:

We

The least important word:

I"

Author Unknown

Colin Powell's Rules

1. "It ain't as bad as you think. It will look better in the morning.

2. Get mad, then get over it.

3. Avoid having your ego so close to your position that when your position falls, your ego goes with it.

4. It can be done!

5. Be careful what you choose. You may get it.

6. Don't let adverse facts stand in the way of a good decision.

7. You can't make someone else's choices. You shouldn't let someone else make yours.

8. Check small things.

9. Share credit.

10. Remain calm. Be kind.

11. Have a vision. Be demanding.

12. Don't take counsel of your fears or naysayers.

13. Perpetual optimism is a force multiplier."

General Colin Powell
Chairman, Joint Chiefs of Staff

Manners

"The first quality of a good education is good manners. Some people flunk the course."

Hubert Humphrey
U.S. Vice President
(To hecklers at a university speech
during the Vietnam War)

"Manners are a sensitive awareness of the feelings of others. If you have that awareness, you have good manners, no matter what fork you use."

Emily Post
Author, Etiquette Advisor

"I have noticed that people who are late are often so much jollier than the people who have to wait for them."

E.V. Lucas
British Author, Essayist

"It's okay to laugh in the bedroom so long as you don't point."

Will Durst
Comedian, Satirist

"It is the duty of every dinner guest to be a good conversationalist."

Oscar Wilde
Irish Dramatist, Wit

"Good manners are not just for sissies."

Title of an article written for the
USMA Cadet Magazine, "Pointer
View" by Bob Moscatelli, circa 1978

"The test of good manners is to be patient with the bad ones."

Gabriol
Occupation Unknown

"The most gracious thing a man can do is to say a kind word to an ugly woman."

Philip Wylie
A Generation of Vipers

"Punctuality is the politeness of kings and the duty of gentle people everywhere."

Unknown

<u>Marriage</u>

"It's got to be more us and less you and me."

Bonnie Moscatelli
Heidelberg, FRG, (3 March 71)

"To keep your marriage brimming
With love in a loving cup,
Whenever you're wrong, admit it,
Whenever you're right, shut up."

Ogden Nash
Humorous Poet

"My wife says I don't listen—at least that's what I think she said."

Unknown

"If you wish to be happy for an hour,
        get intoxicated.
If you wish to be happy for three days,
        get married.
If you wish to be happy for eight days,
        kill your pig and eat it.
If you wish to be happy forever,
        learn to fish."

Chinese Saying

"Women's faults are many.
Men have but two—
Everything they say
            and
Everything they do."

Unknown

"Whether a man ends up with a nest egg or a goose egg, depends upon the kind of chick he marries."

Unknown

"The course of true love never did run smooth."

William Shakespeare
English Playwright

"To marry a second time represents the triumph of hope over experience."

Samuel Johnson
English Author, Critic

"Don't marry the person you think you can live with; marry only the one you think you can't live without."

James Dobson
Founder, Focus on the Family

"There are two theories to arguing with a woman. Neither works."

Will Rogers
Author, Humorist

"Trouble in marriage often starts when a man gets so busy earnin' his salt that he forgets his sugar."

Unknown

"Too many couples marry for better or for worse but not for good."

Unknown

"If a man has enough horse sense to treat his wife like a thoroughbred, she will never turn into an old nag."

Unknown

"A foolish husband says to his wife, 'Honey, you stick to the washin', ironin', cookin' and scrubbin'. No wife of mine is gonna work.'"

Unknown

"The bonds of matrimony are a good investment only when the interest is kept up."

Unknown

"Many girls like to marry a military man. He can cook, sew and make beds and is in good health, and he's already used to taking orders."

Unknown

"I think men who have a pierced ear are better prepared for marriage. They have experienced pain and bought jewelry."

Rita Rudner
Comedian

"It takes two to make a marriage a success but only one to make it a failure."

Herbert Samuel
Author

"I am a marvelous housekeeper. Every time I leave a man, I keep his house."

Zsa Zsa Gabor
Actress

"There's a way of transferring funds that is even faster than electronic banking. It's called marriage."

Donald Mcgannon
President, Westinghouse Corporation

"Instead of getting married again, I'm going to find a woman I don't like and give her a house."

Lewis Grizzard
Newspaper Columnist

"This would be a better world if more married couples were as deeply in love as they are in debt."

Earl Wilson
Journalist

"On anniversaries, the wise husband always forgets the past—but never the present."

Unknown

"I have learned that only two things are necessary to keep one's wife happy. First, let her think she's having her way. And second, let her have it."

Lyndon B. Johnson
U.S. President

"Well-married, a man is winged: ill-matched, he is shackled."

Henry Ward Beecher
Clergyman, Editor

"My ambition is to have a happy home."

Answer given by the Japanese contestant in
the Miss Universe Contest, circa 1965,
when asked her ambition if she were to win.

__Military__

"To those who fight for it, life has a special flavor the protected will never know."

Unknown Soldier, RVN

"Let not the spirit of any man say, had I but had better training I would be alive today."

Unknown

"It is better to have a lion at the head of an army of sheep, than a sheep at the head of an army of lions."

Unknown

"War hath no fury like a noncombatant."

C. F. Montague
Occupation Unknown

"Selfless service, not unbridled ambition, is the proper ethic of the Officer Corps."

Edwin Meyer
General, U. S. Army

"The values necessary to defend the society are often at odds with the values of the society itself."

Walter Kirwin
General, U. S. Army

"What the commander doesn't check doesn't get done."

Bruce Clarke
General, U. S. Army

"Why do these women want to trade the best of what it is to be a woman for the worst of what it is to be a man?"

Marine Colonel in testimony
before a congressional committee
on women in combat arms.

"The maximum effective range of an excuse is zero meters."

U. S. Army Saying

"A soldier's highest accolade is to be honored by other soldiers."

Unknown

"In the social order in which one person is subordinated to another, the superior, if he is a gentleman, never thinks of it and the subordinate, if he is a gentleman, never forgets it."

John Pershing
General, U. S. Army

"It is customary in democratic countries to deplore expenditures on armaments as conflicting with the requirements of social services. There is a tendency to forget that the most important social service that a government can do for its people is to keep them alive and free."

Sir John Slessor
Marshal, Royal Air Force

"If the band played a piece first with the piccolo, then with the brass horn, then with the clarinet and then with the trumpet, there would be a hell of a lot of noise but no music. To get harmony in music, each instrument must support the others. To get harmony in battle, each weapon must support the others. TEAM PLAY WINS."

George S. Patton
General, U. S. Army

"If one side wages war at a cost that is indefinitely acceptable while the other is waging war at a cost that is not indefinitely acceptable, then the former, although losing every battle, is winning the war."

Sir Robert Thompson
Reference the war in Vietnam
Army War College Speech, 16 Sep 77

"As an army, you (the United States) have always excelled at getting there 'firstest with the mostest.' This was a war (RVN) when you had to get there 'longest with the leastest.'"

Sir Robert Thompson
Army War College Speech, 16 Sep 77

"We do our job best when we prevent war not when we fight it."

Colonel Wakin,
Professor of Ethics
U.S. Air Force Academy

"If it be life that awaits, I shall live forever unconquered. If death, I shall die at last strong in my pride and free."

Unknown

"Strategy is only concerned with the problem of winning military victory; grand strategy is concerned with a long view—winning the peace."

Liddel Hart
<u>On War</u>

"Pale Ebenezer thought it wrong to fight….
Ruddy Bill, who killed him, thought it right."

Winston Churchill
British Prime Minister

"I don't mind being called tough, since I find that in this racket, it's the tough guys who lead the survivors."

Curtis LeMay
General, U. S. Air Force

"History does not long entrust the care of freedom to the weak or the timid."

Dwight D. Eisenhower
U. S. President, General

"An army is like spaghetti. You cannot push spaghetti; you must pull it."

George S. Patton
General, U. S. Army

"It is the destiny of the professional soldier to wait in obscurity most of his life for a crisis that may never come. It is his function to know how to solve it if it does come. It is his code to give all that he has."

"Time Magazine", 26 Dec 55
Author Unknown

"Let us have faith that right makes might and in that faith, let us to the end dare to do our duty as we understand it."

Abraham Lincoln
Cooper Union Address

"Since I was a child, I always thought that soldiers died in battle. I never realized that there were so many soldiers and so few battles."

Movie "Beau Geste"

"Never interrupt your enemy when he is making a mistake."

Napoleon Bonaparte
Emperor of France

"Nothing is clearer in history than the adoption by successful rebels of the methods they were accustomed to condemn in the forces they deposed."

Will and Ariel Durant
Lessons of History

"A man who has nothing that he cares about more than his personal safety is a miserable creature who has no chance of being free unless made and kept so by the exertions of better men than himself."

John Stuart Mill
English Philosopher

"If you expect the unexpected and are prepared, then you will never be surprised."

Sun Tzu
Chinese Military Strategist

"Discipline is the training that makes punishment unnecessary."

Robert E. Lee
General
Confederate Army

"The tree of liberty must, from time to time, be watered by the blood of patriots."

Thomas Paine
Political Leader, Theoretician

"People sleep peaceably in their beds at night because rough men stand ready to do violence on their behalf."

George Orwell
Author

"The army is the nation's first line of defense. Wherever the American soldier is stationed along the Iron-Bamboo Curtain, he is a visible obstacle to the aggressor and a source of encouragement to our friends."

Maxwell Taylor
General, U. S. Army

"We have good corporals and sergeants, and some good lieutenants and captains, and those are far more important than good generals."

William T. Sherman
General, Union Army

"This is my rifle. There are many like it, but this one is mine. I must fire my rifle true. I must shoot straighter than my enemy who is trying to kill me. I must shoot him before he shoots me. I will. Before God, I swear this creed. My rifle and myself are the defenders of my country."

Marine Corps Creed

"For as long a time as we can see into the future, we shall be living between a war that cannot be fought and a peace that cannot be achieved. The great issues which divide the world cannot be decided by a war that could be won, and they cannot be settled by a treaty that can be negotiated."

Walter Lippman
Journalist

"An army of stags led by a lion is more to be feared that an army of lions led by a stag."

Chabrias, 400 BC
Athenian General

"Now, I want you to remember that no son-of-a-bitch ever won a war by dying for his country. He won it by making the other poor dumb son-of-a-bitch die for his country."

George S. Patton
General, U. S. Army

"The aggressor is a man of peace. He wants nothing more than to march into a neighbor's country unresisted."

Karl von Clausewitz
German Military Strategist

"God and the soldier we adore,

In time of danger, not before;

The danger passed and all things righted,

God is forgotten, the soldier slighted."

Unknown
Written by a soldier in Napoleon's Army

"When the common soldiers are too strong and their officers too weak, the result is insubordination. When the officers are too strong and the common soldiers too weak, the result is collapse."

Sun Tzu
Chinese Military Strategist

"The acid test of an officer who aspires to high command is his ability to be able to grasp quickly the essentials of a military problem, to decide rapidly what he will do, to make it quite clear to all concerned what he intends to achieve and how he will do it, and then to see that his subordinates get on with the job."

Field Marshal Montgomery
Great Britain

"I divide my officers into four classes: the clever, the stupid, the industrious and the lazy. Every officer possesses at least two of these qualities. Those who are clever and industrious are fitted for high staff appointments; use can be made of those who are stupid and lazy. The man who is clever and lazy is fitted for highest command; he has the temperament and the requisite nerve to deal with all situations. But whoever is stupid and industrious is a danger and must be removed immediately."

Unknown German General

"Regard your soldiers as your children, and they will follow you into the deepest valleys; look at them as your own beloved sons, and they will stand by you even unto death. If, however, you are indulgent, but unable to make your authority felt; kindhearted but unable to enforce your commands; and incapable, moreover, of quelling disorder, then your soldiers must be likened to spoiled children; they are useless for any practical purpose."

Sun Tzu
Chinese Philosopher, General

"Men may be inexact or even untruthful in ordinary matters….but the inexact or untruthful soldier trifles with the lives of his fellowmen, and the honor of his government; and it is, therefore, no matter of idle pride but rather of stern disciplinary necessity that makes West Point require of her students a character for trustworthiness that knows no evasion."

Newton Baker
U. S. Secretary of War

"But an officer on duty knows no one. To be partial is to dishonor both himself and the object of his ill-advised favor. What will be thought of him who winks at and overlooks offenses in one that he causes to be punished in another and contrast him to the inflexible soldier who does his duty notwithstanding it occasionally wars with his private feelings. The conduct of one is to be venerated and emulated, the other detested as a satire upon soldiership and honor."

Brevet Major William Worth
"Worth's Battalion Orders"

"There are no atheists in foxholes."

Unknown

"The discipline that makes the soldiers of a free country reliable in battle is not to be gained by harsh or tyrannical treatment. On the contrary, such treatment is far more likely to destroy than to make an army. It is possible to impart instructions and give commands in such manner and such a tone of voice as to inspire in the soldier no feeling but an intense desire to obey; while the opposite manner and tone of voice cannot fail to excite strong resentment and a desire to disobey. The one mode or the other of dealing with subordinates springs from a corresponding spirit in the breast of the commander. He who feels, and hence manifests, the respect which is due to others cannot fail to inspire in them regard for himself; while he who feels, and hence manifests, disrespect toward others, especially his inferiors, cannot fail to excite hatred against himself."

Major General Schofield
Address to the Corps of Cadets, USMA
West Point, NY August 11, 1879

"And let us remember when all things are said and done, that one great fact, the greatest fact, remains supreme and unassailable. It is this. There are in this world things that are true and things that are false; there are ways that are right and ways that are wrong; there are men good and men bad. On the one side or the other we must take our stand; one or the other we must serve."

Field Marshal Montgomery
Great Britain

"The God of War hates those who hesitate."

Euripides
Greek Dramatist

79

"But I remember when the fight was done,
    When I was dry with rage and extreme toil,
Breathless and faint, leaning upon my sword,
    Came there a certain lord,
Neat and trimly dressed,
    Fresh as a bridegroom.
For he made be mad,
    To see him shine so brisk
And smell so sweet,
    And talk......
Of guns and drums and wounds.
God save the mark!"

William Shakespeare
English Playwright

"The troops I have commanded have always been well dressed, been smart saluters, been prompt and bold in action, because I have personally set the example in these qualities. The influence that one man can have upon thousands is a never ending source of wonder to me. You are always on parade. Officers who, through laziness or a foolish desire to be popular, fail to enforce discipline and proper wearing of equipment not in the presence of the enemy, will also fail in battle; and if they fail in battle, they are potential murderers. There is no such thing as a good field soldier. You are a good soldier or a bad soldier."

George Patton
General, U. S. Army
Letter to his son

"Upon the plains of apathy
   bleach the bones of the victor
   who sat down to rest.
In peace or war man never stops
   ever alert to those dangers
   which beset man as one
   and man as many.
Vigilance is the price which must be paid
   lest slavery of body and soul
   and tyranny o'er the minds of men
Throw the world again into a process of decay."

Unknown

Two Commanders

"Two kinds of commanders, my company needs,
    One for the words, the other for deeds.
One to parade us with guidons held high,
    The other to lead us when steel starts to fly.
One who will push us to get ourselves squared,
    Another to pull us when we get damned scared.
One to inspect us to make us stay clean,
    Another to train us to make us 'real mean.'
A captain who is always starched, pressed and STRIKE,
    A captain whose boots may show wear from our hike.
A leader with ribbons displayed on his shirt,
    A leader whose face will sweat streaks in the dirt.
We need a commander whose accounts are just right,
    We need an 'Old Man' who can teach us to fight.
Would it not fit a magnificent plan,
    If both our commanders could be the same man?"

PFC David B. Farley
A/1-30 Infantry

"Every man thinks meanly of himself for never having been a soldier or not having been to sea."

Samuel Johnson
English Critic, Author

"When you make a decision, you must anticipate all of the possible consequences of that decision and be prepared to deal with them."

General A. Goodpaster
Superintendent, USMA, West Point
Circa 1978
(Paraphrase)

"Five Primary Obligations of a Military Officer

1. *To dedicate his active life to his profession.*
2. *To strive constantly for self-improvement with the ultimate goal the achievement of total fitness—professional, physical, intellectual and moral.*
3. *To set a model of excellence in the performance of duty capable of evoking the confidence and respect of his comrades.*
4. *To demonstrate in word and deed the possession of the cardinal virtues of competence, reliability, justice, courage and determination.*
5. *To make his highest concern the training and well-being of his subordinates."*

General Maxwell Taylor
(Paraphrase)

"I listen vainly, but with thirsty ear, for the witching melody of faint bugles blowing reveille, of far drums beating the long roll. In my dreams I hear again the crash of guns, the rattle of musketry, the strange mournful mutter of the battlefield. But in the evening of my life, I always come back to West Point. Always there echoes and re-echoes in my ears—Duty, Honor, Country. Today marks my final roll call with you. But I want you to know that when I cross the river my last conscious thought will be of the Corps....and the Corps....and the Corps. I bid you farewell."

Gen. Douglas MacArthur
Thayer Award Speech
USMA, West Point, 1962

"Write your orders as though you were a miser sending a prepaid telegram to a fool."

Unknown

The order below was given by Emperor Haille Salaisse of Ethiopia when that nation was struggling for its life against Italian troops in 1935.

"Everyone will now be mobilized!

All boys old enough to carry a spear will be sent to Addis Abbaba.

Married men will take their women to carry food and cook.

Women with small babies need not go.

The blind, those who cannot walk or for any reason cannot carry a spear, are exempted.

Anyone found at home after receipt of this order will be hanged."

> (Haille Salaisse's order is a perfect example of the quote listed directly before it-- short, direct, clear.)

"These are the times that will try men's souls: when the summer soldier and the sunshine patriot will shirk from the performance of his duty."

Thomas Paine
Political Leader
Theoretician

"In peace the sons bury their fathers, but in war the fathers bury their sons."

Croesus
King of Lydia

"Old soldiers never die; they just fade away."

Douglas MacArthur
General, U.S. Army

"I see these things, still am I slave,

When banners flaunt and bugles blow,

Content to fill a soldier's grave,

For reasons I shall never know."

C. T. Lanham
General, U. S. Army

"Anyone who has looked into the glazed eyes of a soldier dying on the battlefield will think hard before starting a war."

Otto Von Bismarck
German Statesman

"When war does come, my advice is to draw the sword and throw away the scabbard."

Thomas "Stonewall" Jackson
General, Army of the Confederacy

"Television brought the brutality of war into the comfort of the living room. Vietnam was lost in the living room of America—not on the battlefields of Vietnam."

Marshall McLuhan
Author

"The higher level of grand strategy is that of conducting war with a far-sighted regard to the state of the peace that will follow."

Liddell Hart
English Author, Military Strategist

"It is fatal to enter any war without the will to finish it."

Douglas MacArthur
General, U.S. Army

"When the enemy advances, withdraw; when he stops, harass; when he tires, strike; when he retreats, pursue."

Mao Tse-tung
Chinese Communist Leader

"Battles are sometimes won by generals; wars are nearly always won by sergeants and privates."

F.E. Adcock
British Scholar

"Lead me, follow me or get out of my way."

George Patton
General, U.S. Army

"There is no type of human endeavor where it is so important that the leader understands all phases of his job as that of the profession of arms."

James Fry
Major General, U.S. Army

"Soldiers will be as lousy as you let them be or as good as you insist that they be. If you tolerate mediocrity, you'll get it."

Bob Moscatelli
Command Philosophy
3rd Brigade, 4th Infantry Division

"Sir, I'd reenlist if you'd get rid of the punks."

A fine young soldier's response when
his brigade commander asked him
why he was not going to reenlist.
Fort Carson, Colorado, 1983

"To be prepared for war is the most effective means of preserving peace."

George Washington
U.S. President

"I am convinced that the best service a retired general can perform is to turn in his tongue along with his suit and to mothball his opinions."

Omar Bradley
General U.S. Army

<u>Opportunity</u>

"We cannot create the opportunity for greatness. That either strikes us or passes us by. We can, however, prepare ourselves against the event of opportunity's finding us unready."

<u>Great Captains Before Napoleon</u>

"The secret to success in life is for a man to be ready for his opportunity when it comes."

Benjamin Disraeli
British Statesman, Author

"If you're looking for a big opportunity, seek out a big problem."

H. Jackson Brown
<u>A Father's Book Of Wisdom</u>

"Opportunity seems to strike at the door of only those men who have prepared themselves for greater things."

Captain M. Rious,
Royal Canadian Army

"Opportunity's favorite disguise is trouble."

Frank Tyger
Occupation Unknown

"Opportunity is missed by most people because it is dressed in overalls and looks like work."

Thomas Edison
Inventor

"In the middle of difficulty lies opportunity."

Albert Einstein
Physicist

"Opportunity may knock once, but temptation leans on the bell."

Unknown

"Each problem has hidden in it an opportunity so powerful that it literally dwarfs the problem. The greatest success stories were created by people who recognized a problem and turned it into an opportunity."

Joseph Sugarman
Author

<u>Optimism</u>

"Keep your face to the sunshine, and the shadows will fall behind you."

Walt Whitman
Poet

"When the road is long, one must look at the horizon and not at the dust at his feet."

Ralph Waldo Emerson
Philosopher, Poet

"Twixt the optimist and the pessimist, the difference is droll. The optimist sees the doughnut, the pessimist the hole."

McLandburgh Wilson
Writer

"Two men look out through the same bars: one sees mud, and one the stars."

Frederick Langbridge
British Author

"When everything else seems to have failed, there's nothing wrong with a little hope."

Dr. Bernie Siegel
Oncologist
<u>Peace, Love and Healing</u>

"What the mind of man can conceive and believe, the mind of man can achieve."

Napoleon Hill
Think And Grow Rich

"A poor person who is unhappy is in a better position than a rich person who is unhappy. Because the poor person has hope. He thinks money would help."

John Kerr
Poor Richard

"The pessimist looks at opportunities and sees difficulties. The optimist looks at difficulties and sees opportunities."

Unknown

Poems

Forget Yesterday

"I am where I am.
I know where I could have been,
Had I done what I did not do.
Tell me, friend, what I can do today,
To be where I want to be tomorrow."

Sigrad
Occupation Unknown

Getting A Good Deal

"When you're getting a bargain,
Remember what is real,
Is that the person you're getting the bargain from,
Thinks he's getting the better of the deal."

Harold Helfer
Occupation Unknown

"Bullfight critics ranked in rows,
Crowd the enormous plaza full;
But only one man is there who knows,
And he's the man who fights the bull."

Domingo Ortega
Spanish Dancer

"It is not the guns or armament or the money they can pay,
It's the close cooperation that makes them win the day.
It is not the individual or the Army as a whole,
But the everlasting teamwork of every bloomin' soul."

J. Mason Knox
Soldier, 24th Infantry Regiment
U. S. Army, 1898

Don't You Quit

"Success is failure turned inside out,
The silver tint of the clouds of doubt.
And you never can tell how close you are,
It may be near when it seems so far.
So stick to the fight when you're hardest hit,
It's when things seem worse,
That you must not quit."

Unknown

"Mine is not to run this train,
The whistle I can't blow.
Mine is not to say
How far this train can go.
I'm not allowed to blow off steam
Or even ring the bell;
But let this train run off the track
And see who catches hell."

Unknown

"There is a destiny that makes us brothers,
None goes his way alone.
That which we put into the lives of others,
Comes back into our own."

Edwin Markham
Poet

"I shall be telling this with a sigh
Somewhere ages and ages hence:
Two roads diverged in a wood, and I—
I took the one less traveled by,
And that has made all the difference."

Robert Frost
Poet

High Flight

"Oh, I have slipped the surly bonds of earth
And danced the skies on laughter-silvered wings.
Sunward I've climbed and joined the tumbling mirth,
The sun-split clouds, and done a hundred things
You have not dreamed of.
Wheeled and soared and swung high in the sunlit
     silence.
Hovering there, I've chased the shouting wind along
And flung my eager craft through footless halls of air.
Up, up, delirious along burning blue,
I've topped the windswept heights with easy grace
Where never lark or even eagle flew.
And while with silent lifting mind, I've trod
The high untrespassed sanctity of space
Put out my hand and touched the face of God."

John Gillespie McGee, Jr.
American Pilot with RAF
World War II

The Man Who Thinks He Can

"If you think you are beaten, you are;
If you think you dare not, you don't.
If you like to win, but you think you can't,
It's almost certain you won't.

If you think you'll lose, you're lost,
For out in the world we find,
Success begins with a fellow's will,
It's all in the state of mind.

If you think you're outclassed, you are,
You've got to think high to rise,
You've got to be sure of yourself before
You can ever win the prize.

Life's battles do not always go
To the stronger or faster man,
But soon or late the man who wins
Is the man who thinks he can."

Walter Wintle
Poet

"If for a tranquil mind you seek,
   These things observe with care:
Of whom you speak, to whom you speak,
   And how, and when and where."

"A wise old owl sat on an oak,
   The more he heard, the less he spoke.
The less he spoke, the more he heard,
   Why aren't we all like that wise old bird?"

Unknown

__Prayer__

Abby's Blessing
Abigail Van Buren

"Oh, Heavenly Father:
We thank Thee for food and remember the hungry,
We thank Thee for health and remember the sick,
We thank Thee for friends and remember the friendless,
We thank Thee for freedom and remember the enslaved.
May these remembrances stir us to service,
That Thy gifts to us may be used for others."

American Indian Prayer
"Great Spirit: Grant that I may not criticize my neighbor until I have walked a mile in his moccasins."

Irish Blessing
"May the road rise up to meet you;
May the wind always be at your back;
May the sun shine warm upon your face
And the rain fall soft upon your fields.
And, until we meet again,
May God hold you in the palm of His hands."

"Lord, we thank Thee for Thy many gifts, we ask just one thing more—a grateful heart."

Unknown

"Prayer: To ask the laws of the universe be annulled on behalf of a single petitioner, confessedly unworthy."

Ambrose Bierce
Author

Growing Older

17th Century Nun's Prayer

"Lord, Thou knowest better than I know myself that I am growing older and will some day be old. Keep me from getting talkative, and particularly from the fatal habit of thinking that I must say something on every occasion. Release me from the craving to straighten out everybody's affairs. Keep my mind free from the recital of endless details—give me wings to get to the point. I ask for grace enough to listen to the tales of other's pains. Help me to endure them with patience. But seal my own lips on my own aches and pains—they are increasing and my love of rehearsing them is becoming sweeter. Teach me the glorious lesson that occasionally it is possible that I may be mistaken. Keep me reasonably sweet; I do not want to be a Saint—some of them are so hard to live with—but a sour old woman or man is one of the crowning works of the devil. Make me thoughtful, but not moody; helpful, but not bossy. With my vast store of wisdom, it seems a pity not to use it all, but Thou knowest, Lord, I want a few friends at the end."

I Asked God

"I asked God for strength that I might achieve;

I was made weak that I might learn humbly to obey.

I asked for health that I might do greater things;

I was given infirmity that I might do better things.

I asked for riches that I might be happy;

I was given poverty that I might be wise.

I asked for power that I might have the praise of men;

I was given weakness that I might feel the need of God.

I asked for all things that I might enjoy life;

I was given life that I might enjoy all things.

I got nothing that I asked for but everything that I had hoped for.

Almost despite myself, my unspoken prayers were answered.

I am, among all men, most richly blessed."

Author Unknown

Cadet Prayer
United States Military Academy

"God, our Father, Thou Searcher of men's hearts, help us to draw near to Thee in sincerity and truth. May our religion be filled with gladness and may our worship of Thee be natural.

Strengthen and increase our admiration for honest dealing and clean thinking and suffer not our hatred of hypocrisy and pretense ever to diminish. Encourage us in our endeavor to live above the common level of life. Make us to choose the harder right instead of the easier wrong, and never to be content with a half truth when the whole can be won. Endow us with courage that is born of loyalty to all that is noble and worthy, that scorns to compromise with vice and injustice, and knows no fear when truth and right are in jeopardy. Guard us against flippancy and irreverence in the sacred things of life. Grant us new ties of friendship and new opportunities of service. Kindle our hearts with fellowship with those of a cheerful countenance, and soften our hearts with sympathy with those who sorrow and suffer. Help us to maintain the honor of the Corps untarnished and unsullied and to show forth in our lives the ideals of West Point in doing our duty to Thee and to our country. All of which we ask in the name of the Great Friend and Master of Men. Amen"

"O, do not pray for easy lives. Pray to be stronger men. Do not pray for tasks equal to your prowess. Pray for prowess equal to your tasks."

Phillip Brooks
Protestant Bishop

This prayer was given by Reverend Joe Wright at the opening of a new session of the Kansas Senate:

"Heavenly Father, we come before you today to ask Your forgiveness and to seek Your direction and guidance. We know Your Word says, 'Woe unto those who call evil good,' but that is exactly what we have done. We have lost our spiritual equilibrium and reversed our values.

We confess that we have ridiculed the absolute truth of Your Word and called it pluralism.

We have worshipped other gods and called it multiculturalism.

We have endorsed perversion and called it an alternate lifestyle.

We have exploited the poor and called it the lottery.

We have rewarded laziness and called it welfare.

We have killed our unborn and called it choice.

We have shot abortionists and called it justifiable.

We have neglected to discipline our children and called it building self-esteem.

We have abused power and called it politics.

We have coveted our neighbors possessions and called it ambition.

We have polluted the air with profanity and pornography and called it freedom of expression.

We have ridiculed the time-honored values of our forefathers and called it enlightenment.

Search us, Oh God, and know our hearts today; cleanse us from every sin and set us free. Guide and bless these men and women who have been sent to direct us to the center of Your will. I ask it in the name of Your Son, the living Savior, Jesus Christ, Amen."

__Presidents/Politicians__

"Ask not what your country can do for you. Ask what you can do for your country."

John F. Kennedy
U. S. President

"Drift is the demon of democracy."

Anthony Eden
British Prime Minister

"You cannot strengthen the weak by weakening the strong.

You cannot help the poor by destroying the rich.

You cannot help men permanently by doing for them what they could or should do for themselves."

Abraham Lincoln
U. S. President

"Let every nation know, whether it wishes us well or ill, we shall pay any price, bear any burden, meet any hardship, support any friend, oppose any foe to assure the survival and the success of liberty."

John F. Kennedy
U. S. President

"The right to freedom of speech does not give anyone the right to yell 'fire' in a crowded theater."

Oliver Wendel Holmes
Lawyer, Jurist

"If you can't take the heat, stay out of the kitchen."

Harry S. Truman
U. S. President

"Any dangerous spot is tenable if brave men will make it so."

John F. Kennedy
U. S. President

"If a politician found he had cannibals among his constituents, he would promise them missionaries for dinner."

H.L. Mencken
Satirist, Social Critic

"Here's my strategy on the Cold War: We win, they lose."

Ronald Reagan
U. S. President

"Nearly all men can stand adversity, but if you want to test a man's character, give him power."

Abraham Lincoln
U. S. President

"In whatever arena of life one may meet the challenge of courage, whatever may be the sacrifices he faces if he follows his conscience—the loss of his friends, his fortune, his contentment, even the esteem of his fellow men—each man must decide for himself the course he will follow."

John F. Kennedy
U. S. President

Washington, having been asked by an officer on the morning of a battle what were his plans for the day, replied in a whisper, "Can you keep a secret?" On being answered in the affirmative, the general added, "So can I."

George Washington
U. S. President

"Inconsistencies of opinion arising from changes in circumstances are often justifiable. But there is one sort of inconsistency that is culpable: it is the inconsistency between a man's conviction and his vote, between his conscience and his conduct. No man shall ever charge me with an inconsistency of that kind."

Daniel Webster
U. S. Diplomat

"The reason there are so few female politicians is that it is too much trouble to put makeup on two faces."

Maureen Murphy
Occupation Unknown

"No person was ever honored for what he received. Honor has been the reward for what he gave."

Calvin Coolidge
U. S. President

"It has been my experience that folks who have no vices have very few virtues."

Abraham Lincoln
U. S. President

"The complacent, the self-indulgent, the soft societies are to be swept away with the debris of history; only the strong, only the industrious, only the visionary can survive."

John F. Kennedy
U.S. President

"For all its blemishes, the United States stands in the forefront of the world in its commitment to the proposition that the individual human being should be free—free to think what he wants, write what he wishes, assemble as he will, read as his curiosity leads him, paint as his eye uniquely sees, worship as to him seems right, and espouse whatsoever political position he finds congenial, so long only as he accords those same privileges to his fellow citizens."

Bayless Manning
"Foreign Affairs", (Jan '76)

"A monarchy or despotism is like a full rigged sailing ship. It moves swiftly and efficiently. It is beautiful to behold. It responds sharply to the helm. But in troubled waters when it strikes a rock, its shell is pierced and it quickly sinks to the bottom. A republic, however, is like a raft: slow, ungainly, impossible to steer, no place from which to control events, and yet endurable and safe. It will not sink, but one's feet are always wet."

Fisher Ames
Congressman from Massachusetts

"The whole aim of practical politics is to keep the populace alarmed (and hence clamorous to be led to safety) by menacing it with an endless series of hobgoblins, all of them imaginary."

H.L. Mencken
Satirist, Social Critic

"Of the four wars in my lifetime, none came about because the United States was too strong."

Ronald Reagan
U. S. President

"If I were to try to read, much less answer, all the attacks made on me, this shop might as well be closed for any other business. I do the very best I know how, the very best I can, and I mean to keep on doing so until the end. If the end brings me out all right, what is said against me won't amount to anything. If the end brings me out wrong, ten thousand angels swearing I was right would make no difference."

Abraham Lincoln
U. S. President

"In politics, if you want something said, ask a man. If you want something done, ask a woman."

Margaret Thatcher
British Prime Minister

"I have wondered at times about what the Ten Commandments would look like if Moses had run them through the U. S. Congress."

Ronald Reagan
U. S. President

"It is not the critic who counts, nor the man who points out where the strong man stumbled, or where the doer of deeds could have done them better. The credit belongs to the man who is actually in the arena, whose face is marred by dust and sweat and blood; who strives valiantly, who errs and comes short again and again, who knows the great enthusiasms, the great devotions and spends himself in a worthy cause; who, at the worst, if he fails, at least fails while daring greatly so that his place shall never be with those cold and timid souls who know neither victory nor defeat."

Theodore Roosevelt
U. S. President

"The trouble with our liberal friends is not that they're ignorant. It's just that they know so much that isn't so."

Ronald Reagan
U. S. President

"History does not long entrust the care of freedom to the weak or the timid."

Dwight D. Eisenhower
U. S. President

"I would rather go down to my political grave with a clear conscience than ride in the chariot of victory—a stool pigeon, the slave, the servant, or the vassal of any man, whether he be the owner and manager of a legislative menagerie or the ruler of a great nation. I would rather lie in the silent grave, remembered by both friends and enemies as one who remained true to his faith and who never faltered in what he believed to be his duty, than to still live, old and aged, lacking the confidence of both factions."

George W. Norris
U. S. Senator

"It is inaccurate to say that I hate everything. I am strongly in favor of common sense, common honesty and common decency. That makes me forever ineligible for public office."

H. L. Mencken
Satirist, Social Critic

"I watched a small man with thick calluses on both hands work 15 or 16 hours a day. I saw a man who came here uneducated, alone, unable to speak the language, who taught me all I needed to know about faith and hard work by the simple eloquence of his example."

Mario Cuomo
Governor of New York

"We must be willing, individually and as a nation, to accept whatever sacrifices may be required of us. A people that values its privileges above its principles soon loses both."

Dwight D. Eisenhower
U. S. President

"The probability that we may fail in the struggle ought not to deter us from the support of a cause we believe to be just."

Abraham Lincoln
U. S. President

"I would rather lose in a cause I know someday will triumph, than win in a cause that I know someday will fail."

Woodrow Wilson
U.S. President

Proverbs

"A society grows great when old men plant trees whose shade they know they will never sit in."

Greek

"It is better to live one day as a lion than a hundred years as a sheep."

Italian

"A voyage of a thousand miles begins with a single step."

Chinese

"The water downstream cannot be clear, if the water upstream is muddy."

Korean

"When the king makes a mistake, all the people suffer."

Chinese

"Fear knocked at the door. Faith answered. No one was there."

English

"Repetition is the mother of learning (and the father of boredom)."

Russian

"One look is worth a thousand reports."

Japanese

"Fortune favors the bold but abandons the timid."

Latin

"Smooth seas do not make skillful sailors."

African

"Whoever gossips to you will gossip of you."

Spanish

"Before borrowing money from a friend, decide which you need most."

American

"La vida es un fandango y cuando se es joven, debe bailar."

"Life is a fandango and while one is young, he must dance."

Spanish

"The man who can't dance thinks the band is no good."

Polish

"The admission of ignorance is the first step toward wisdom."

The Bible

"If you can't bite, don't show your teeth."

Yiddish

"Don't buy the house; buy the neighborhood."

Russian

"God gave man two ears and one tongue, so he could listen twice as much as he talked."

Arab

"People count up the faults of those who are keeping them waiting."

French

"Riches serve a wise man but command a fool."

English

"When spider webs unite, they can tie up a lion."

Ethiopian

"Be not afraid of going slowly; be afraid only of standing still."

Chinese

"Do not remove a fly from your friend's forehead with a hatchet."

Chinese

"I was angered for I had no shoes. Then I met a man who had no feet."

Chinese

"A lazy man is never lucky."

Persian

"When the mouse laughs at the cat, there's a hole nearby."

Nigerian

"He who is outside his door already has the hard part of his journey behind him."

Dutch

"Visits always give pleasure—if not the arrival, the departure."

Portuguese

116

"Listen or thy tongue will keep you deaf."

American Indian

"It's a sad house where the hen crows louder than the cock."

Scottish

"When you go to buy, use your eyes, not your ears."

Czech

"Use soft words and hard arguments."

English

"Call on God, but row away from the rocks."

Indian

"You've got to do your own growing, no matter how tall your grandfather was."

Irish

"If you scatter thorns, don't go barefoot."

Italian

"Drink nothing without seeing it; sign nothing without reading it."

Spanish

"Some men go through a forest and see no firewood."

English

"What I hear, I forget;
What I see, I remember;
What I do, I understand."

Chinese

"When you see the teeth of a lion, don't assume that the lion is smiling."

Iraqi

"If you stand straight, do not fear a crooked shadow."

Chinese

__Religion__

"Going to church doesn't make you a good Christian any more than going into a garage makes you a good automobile."

Reverend Billy Graham
Evangelist
USMA, West Point, NY 1958

"Every evening I turn my worries over to God, because he's going to be up all night anyway."

Unknown

"If you're not closer to the Lord today than you were yesterday, guess who moved."

Unknown

"I believe in God on blind faith, not because the Bible told me to."

Reverend Billy Graham
Evangelist
USMA, West Point, NY 1958

"Do not pray for an easy life. Pray to be a strong person."

Unknown

"The road to hell is paved with good intentions."

Unknown

"It's going to be fun to watch and see how long the meek can keep the earth after they inherit it."

Frank Hubbard
Occupation Unknown

Retirement/Growing Older

"If I had known that I would live this long, I would have taken better care of myself."

Eubie Blake
Jazz Pianist, Composer

"Thirty-five is when you finally get your head together and your body starts falling apart."

Caryn Leschen
Occupation Unknown

"Retirement is when you stop living at work and start working at living."

Unknown

"Old age ain't no place for sissies."

Bette Davis
Actress

"Que bonito es hacer nada y, despues de hacer nada, descansar."

"How beautiful it is to do nothing and, after doing nothing, to rest."

Mexican Saying

"Eventually you will get to the point when you stop lying about your age and start bragging about it."

Unknown

"The older we get, the fewer things seem worth waiting in line for."

Unknown

"I'm not afraid to die. I just don't want to be there when it happens."

Woody Allen
Actor, Comedian

"We do not grow old. We become old by not growing."

Unknown

"We get too soon old and too late smart."

Pennsylvania Dutch Saying

"If a man dies and leaves his estate in an uncertain condition, the lawyers become his heirs."

E. W. Howe
Author

"I don't want to achieve immortality through my work. I want to achieve it through not dying."

Woody Allen
Actor, Comedian

"Old people are accused of being forgetful, but they never forget where they have put their money."

Oliver Wendell Holmes
Author, Essayist

"How old would you be if you didn't know how old you are?"

Unknown

<u>Risk</u>

"If you want to sail big ships, you have to go into deep water."

Unknown

"Why not go out on a limb? Isn't that where the fruit is?"

Frank Scully
Educator

"To try when there is little hope is to risk failure. Not trying at all is to guarantee it."

Unknown

"Behold the turtle. He makes progress only when he sticks his neck out."

James Conant
Educator

"During the first period of a man's life the greatest danger is not to take the risk."

Soren Kierkegaard
Danish Philosopher

"He that leaveth nothing to chance will do few things ill, but he will do very few things."

George Savile
English Statesman

"The policy of being too cautious is the greatest risk of all."

Jawaharlal Nehru
Indian Prime Minister

"Do not follow where the path may lead. Go instead where there is no path and leave a trail."

Ralph Waldo Emerson
Philosopher, Poet

"Don't be afraid to take a big step when one is indicated. You can't cross a chasm in two small steps."

David Lloyd George
British Prime Minister

"Progress always involves risk. You can't steal second with your foot on first."

Anonymous

"Take calculated risks. That is quite different from being rash."

George S. Patton
General, U. S. Army

"He either fears his fate too much or his deserts are small, who dares not put it to the touch to win or lose it all."

James Graham
Poet

Success/Failure

"I cannot give you the formula for success, but I can give you the formula for failure, which is—to try to please everybody."

Herbert Swope
Editor, Journalist

"Being defeated is a temporary condition. Giving up is what makes it permanent."

Marlene vos Savant
Columnist

"The Lord gave you two ends—one for sitting and one for thinking. Your success depends on which you use. Heads, you win. Tails, you lose."

Unknown

"If your ship doesn't come in, swim out to it."

Jonathan Winters
Comedian

"If you want to soar with eagles, don't hang around with turkeys."

Unknown

"Success is a journey, not a destination."

Unknown

"I am not judged by the number of times I fail, but by the number of times I succeed, and the number of times I succeed is in direct proportion to the number of times I can fail and keep trying."

Tom Hopkins
Author, Sales Trainer

"When everything goes right, no one remembers; but when something goes wrong, no one forgets."

Unknown

"He has achieved success who has lived well, laughed often and loved much."

Bessie Anderson Stanley
Poet

"If you say it can't be done, you're right. You can't do it."

Unknown

"A man can fail many times, but he isn't a failure until he gives up."

Unknown

"Set and maintain high standards: If you aim low, you can only hit the bulls eye with a ricochet."

Unknown

"Success seems to be largely a matter of hanging on after others have let go."

William Feather
Naturalist, Photographer

"If you have tried to do something and failed, you are vastly better off than if you had tried to do nothing and succeeded."

Unknown

"Success can also come from getting along with people you can't get ahead of."

Unknown

"If there is any one secret of success, it lies in the ability to get the other person's point of view and see things from his angle as well as from your own."

Unknown

"Any failure will tell you that success is nothing but luck."

H.Jackson Brown
A Father's Book of Wisdom

"Rather fail with honor than succeed by fraud."

Sophocles
Greek Philosopher

"Try not to become a man of success but rather to become a man of value."

Albert Einstein
Physicist

"Always bear in mind that your own resolution to succeed is more important than any one thing."

Abraham Lincoln
U. S. President

"Real success is finding your lifework in the work that you love."

David McCullough
Author

"The ladder to success is never crowded at the top."

Napoleon Hill
<u>Think and Grow Rich</u>

"The dictionary is the only place where success comes before work."

Arthur Brisbane
Author

"Failure is often that early morning hour of darkness which precedes the dawning of the day of success."

Leigh Mitchell Hodges
Poet
"Success"

"Before everything else, getting ready is the secret to success."

Henry Ford
Industrialist

"It is amazing what you can accomplish if you don't care who gets the credit."

Harry S. Truman
U. S. President

<u>Time</u>

"I still find each day too short for all the thoughts I want to think, all the walks I want to take, all the books I want to read and all the friends I want to see."

Unknown

"Today is the tomorrow you worried about yesterday."

Unknown

"A sobering thought: You are now living the good old days."

Unknown

"He who has one watch always knows what time it is. He who has two is never sure."

Unknown

"We should all be concerned about the future because we will have to spend the rest of our lives there."

Charles Kettering
Engineer, Inventor

"Punctuality is a virtue recognized by superiors."

Colin Powell
Assistant Division Commander
4th Infantry Division, 1982

<u>Wealth/Money/Investing</u>

"The real secret to being rich is to maintain a good balance as you live your life between making a living and living itself."

Jim Rohn
Motivational Speaker

"Do not rely on Prince Charming to keep you safe."

Jane Bryant Quinn
Financial Columnist
(Financial advice for women)

"We have no more right to consume happiness without producing it than to consume wealth without producing it."

George Bernard Shaw
English Essayist, Critic

"The shortest and best way to make your fortune is to let people see clearly that it is in their interests to promote yours."

Jean de La Bruyere
Occupation Unknown

"Our wealth is in our friends."

Bonnie Moscatelli
May, 1995

"If you would know the value of money, go out and try to borrow some."

Benjamin Franklin
Statesman, Author, Scientist

"If only God would give me some clear sign—like making a large deposit in my name in a Swiss bank."

Woody Allen
Comedian

"The secret to financial success—spend what is left after saving.

The secret to financial failure—save what is left after spending."

USPA & IRA Principle

"It is not what you make that's important, it's what you keep."

Unknown

"Perhaps the one thing worse than dying is outliving your money."

Advertisement
Prudential Securities

"When is the best time to invest? When you have the money."

Bernard Baruch
Financier

"There is no greater blunder than he who consumes the greater part of his life getting his living."

Henry David Thoreau
Essayist

"Forget about a return on my investment. I want a return of my investment."

Will Rogers
Humorist, Author

"What does a broker get when he gives bad advice? A commission."

Advertisement
Quick and Reilly, Inc
Discount Brokers

"Money is a terrible master but an excellent servant."

P. T. Barnum
Showman, Businessman

"Inflation is not all bad. After all, it has allowed every American to live in a more expensive neighborhood without moving."

Alan Cranston
U. S. Senator

"There are two times in a man's life when he shouldn't speculate: when he can't afford it and when he can."

Mark Twain
Author, Humorist

"A reminder to everyone spending like there is no tomorrow: there is a tomorrow."

Advertisement
Chase Manhattan Bank

"When a fellow says it h'aint the money but the principle o' the thing, it's the money."

Frank Hubbard
Humorist, Cartoonist

"All things are cheap to the saving, dear to the wasteful."

Benjamin Franklin
Statesman, Author, Scientist

"There is a way to make a lot of money in the stock market. Unfortunately, it is the same way to lose a lot of money in the market."

P. Passell and L. Rose
Occupations Unknown

"Time itself, rather than timing or guessing market action, is the secret to investment success."

The Johnson's Charts

"When starting out, don't worry about not having enough money. Limited funds are a blessing not a curse. Nothing encourages creative thinking in quite the same way."

H. Jackson Brown
Life's Little Instruction Book

"The number one rule of building wealth is that you must not lose what you already have."

Mark Skonsen
Financial Writer

"Time is the fertilizer of money."

Vaneta Van Caspel
Power of Money Dynamics

"The surest way to achieve your reasonable financial goals is to get on a proven low-risk path early and stay on it."

Bob Moscatelli
Too Soon Old, Too Late Smart

"Bulls can make money and bears can make money, but pigs get slaughtered."

Old Wall Street Adage
Author Unknown

"If you want to earn more than you get, you need to be worth more than you are paid."

Unknown

"Save and earn interest, don't borrow and pay it."

Benjamin Franklin
Statesman, Author, Scientist

"Take care of the pence and the pounds will take care of themselves."

Lord Chesterfield
Statesman, Author

"Americans are getting stronger. Thirty years ago, it took two people to carry ten dollars' worth of groceries. Today, a five-year-old can do it."

Henny Youngman
Comedian

"There is hardly anything in this world that someone cannot make a little cheaper and a little worse, and the people who consider price alone are this man's lawful prey."

John Ruskin
English Writer, Critic

"Part of all you earn is yours to keep."

George Clason
Richest Man In Babylon

"The only difference between death and taxes is that death doesn't get worse every time Congress meets."

Will Rogers
Humorist, Writer

"People who complain about the tax system fall into two categories—men and women."

Barry Steiner
Pay Less Tax Legally

"If you have money, you control your circumstances. If you don't have money, your circumstances control you."

Richard Bolles
What Color Is Your Parachute?

"Beware of little expenses. A small leak will sink a great ship."

Benjamin Franklin
Statesman, Author, Scientist

"If you don't know who you are, Wall Street is an expensive place to find out."

Adam Smith
The Money Game

"Only by living on less than you make will you ever be able to live on more than you make."

Jane Bryant Quinn
Author, Financial Columnist

"Saving is a very fine thing. Especially when your parents have done it for you."

Winston Churchill
British Prime Minister

"So called 'hot tips' and 'sure things' have put more people on the bottom than Nazi U-boats ever did."

Louis Rukeyser
Economic Commentator

"Don't gamble! Take all savings and buy some good stock and wait till it goes up, then sell it. If it don't go up, don't buy it."

Will Rogers
Humorist, Writer

"I've been rich and I've been poor. Believe me, rich is better."

Sophie Tucker
Entertainer

"Creditors have better memories than debtors."

Unknown

"What good is having more than enough money if you have less than enough time?"

Bob Moscatelli
Too Soon Old, Too Late Smart

"He who knows he has enough is rich."

Tao Te Ching
Chinese Philosopher

"A budget tells us what we can't afford, but it doesn't keep us from buying it."

William Feather
Naturalist, Photographer

"No matter how rich you become, how famous or powerful, when you die the size of your funeral will pretty much depend upon the weather."

Michael Pritchard
Author

"If all the economists in the world were laid end to end, they still couldn't reach a conclusion."

Louis Rukeyser
Economic Commentator

"Be brave when everyone is afraid and afraid when everyone is brave."

Warren Buffet
Legendary Investor
(His Success Formula)

"It isn't a question of whether you want to invest or not….. you have to invest…..you have to invest to: Protect your capital against inflation and participate in the growth of the economy. The only question is HOW?"

The Johnson's Charts

"Neither a borrower nor a lender be."

William Shakespeare
English Playwright
"Hamlet"

"There is never a bad time to make a good investment."

Unknown

"A fool and his money are soon parted."

Unknown

"Inflation is a robber. It robs you of purchasing power."

Unknown

"Plastic ought to serve a single purpose: convenience. You put it down instead of writing a check or paying cash. At the end of the month, you pay the bill—the whole bill."

Jane Bryant Quinn
Author, Financial Columnist

"Spend less than you earn and do it for a long time, and you will be financially successful."

Ron Blue
<u>Master Your Money</u>

"Bulls and bears aren't responsible for as many stock losses as bum steers."

Olin Miller
Author

"Inflation is the one form of taxation that can be imposed without legislation."

Milton Friedman
Economist

"Don't just learn how to earn. Learn how to live."

Jim Rohn
"If You Want To Be The Best"
Audiotape

"When a person with money meets a person with experience, the person with experience winds up with the money and the person with money winds up with the experience."

Unknown

"In making an investment decision, the important factor is not what it costs. You do not care what it costs, but you are truly concerned with what it pays."

Vaneta Van Caspel
The Power of Money Dynamics

"It's one of the ironies of retirement planning that the people in the best position to save are middle aged—yet the time to start saving is when you're young."

Andrew Tobias
Financial Writer

"The rich don't really live longer. It just seems like it when you're waiting for the inheritance."

Unknown

"We're all very rich here in Gaylord (Michigan). We have the lakes, the deer, the fish and the trees."

> Owner of the Heidelberg Restaurant in Gaylord when asked, "How many (obviously successful) restaurants like this do you own?" His reply, "Just one." "If you owned more than one, you'd be a very rich man," I observed. His response is quoted above.

<u>Winning/Victory</u>

"The will to win means nothing unless you have the will to prepare."

Kenyan Runner
After winning the NYC Marathon
November 1990

"At the Olympic Games, it is not the finest and strongest men who are crowned, but they who enter the lists—for out of these the prize-men are selected. So, too, in life, of the honorable and the good, it is they who act who rightly win the prizes."

Aristotle
Greek Philosopher

"When the One Great Scorer comes to write against your name, He marks, not that you won or lost, but how you played the game."

Grantland Rice
Sportswriter

"If winning is not important, why do they keep score?"

Unknown

"As always, victory finds a hundred fathers, but defeat is an orphan."

Count Galeazzo Ciano
Occupation Unknown

"Upon the fields of friendly strife are sown the seeds that, on other days and other fields, will bear the fruits of victory."

Douglas MacArthur
General, U. S. Army

"From the Far East, I bring you one single thought, one sole idea written in red on every beachhead from Australia to Tokyo, there is no substitute for victory."

Douglas MacArthur
General, U. S. Army

"Winners are always trying to find time to do more when losers are always trying to find excuses to do less."

Ron Hale
Occupation Unknown

"Be ashamed to die unless you have won some victory for humanity."

Horace Mann
Lawyer, Educator

<u>Work</u>

"I am a great believer in luck, and I find that the harder I work, the more I have of it."

Thomas Jefferson
U. S. President

"Cream doesn't rise to the top. It works its way up."

Unknown

"Pray for a good harvest, but keep on plowing."

Unknown

"The best plan on earth will not work unless you do."

Unknown

"The man who is rowing the boat has no time to rock it."

Unknown

"It's always been and always will be the same in the world: the horse does the work and the coachman is tipped."

Anonymous

"Nothing is really work unless you would rather be doing something else."

James Barrie
Scottish Writer

"You cannot plow the field by turning it over in your mind."

Unknown

"People who want milk shouldn't sit on a stool in the middle of a field in the hopes that a cow will back up to them."

Curtis Grant
Author

"Hard work is the best investment a man can make."

Charles Schwab
Founder, Discount Brokerage

"If you want to make an easy job seem mighty hard, just keep putting off doing it."

Olin Miller
Author

"Work spares us from three great evils: boredom, vice and need."

Voltaire
French Statesman, Dramatist
"Candide"

"As a cure for worrying, work is better than whiskey."

Thomas Edison
Inventor

"So many people like golf because it's the only endeavor that rewards you for a performance that's under par."

Unknown

"Hard work without talent is a shame, but talent without hard work is a tragedy."

Robert Half
Motivational Speaker

The first edition of <u>The Quote Manual</u> was published in 2005 as a fifty-year collection. Since then, I have encountered additional quotes with which I am impressed, and I consider worthy of passing on in this work. If I simply added the recently acquired quotes in the appropriate chapters of the original book, <u>The Quote Manual</u> would no longer be a fifty-year collection. So, the additional quotes, appropriately categorized, are listed in the addendum which follows.

Addendum

Potpourri

"We can easily forgive a child who is afraid of the dark. What is really a tragedy is a man who is afraid of the light."

Criminal Minds
"The Boogyman"
TV Program, 25 Oct 07

"There is no disguise that can long conceal love where it exists or simulate it where it does not."

Francois
Duc de La Rochefoucauld

"I've learned that people will forget what you said, people will forget what you did, but people will never forget how you made them feel."

Maya Angelou
Poet

"A pat on the back, though only a few vertebrae removed from a kick in the pants, is miles ahead in results."

Bennett Cerf
Author

"My father gave me the greatest gift anyone could give another person. He believed in me."

Jim Valvano
Basketball Coach
North Carolina State

"Aggressive fighting for the right is the greatest sport in the world."

Theodore Roosevelt
U. S. President

"The mind of a bigot is like the pupil of the eye; the more light you pour upon it, the more it will contract."

Oliver W. Holmes
Author, Essayist

"Words that soak into your ears are whispered....not yelled."

Unknown

"Don't go around saying the world owes you a living. The world owes you nothing. It was here first."

Mark Twain
Author

"Modesty is the only sure bait when you're fishing for praise."

Gil Chesterton
Radio Host

"Commencement speeches were invented largely in the belief that outgoing college students should never be released into the world until they have been properly sedated."

Garry Trudeau
Prime Minister
Canada

"The quality of a person's life is in direct proportion to their commitment to excellence, regardless of their chosen field of endeavor."

Vince Lombardi
Football Coach
Green Bay Packers

"A crowded elevator smells different to a midget."

Unknown
See Paragraph 5, Page 6

"If we escape punishment for our vices, why should we complain if we are not rewarded for our virtues?"

John Churton Collins
English Author, Lecturer

"It takes a woman twenty years to make a man of her son, and another woman twenty minutes to make a fool of him."

Helen Rowland
Author

"The most important thing a father can do for his children is to love their mother."

Theodore Hesburgh
President
University of Notre Dame

"Never fight with someone who buys ink by the barrel."

Unknown

"We have to be careful in this era of radical feminism, not to emphasize an equality of the sexes that leads women to imitate men to prove their equality. To be equal does not mean you have to be the same."

General Eva Burrows
International Leader
Salvation Army

"You can't build a reputation on what you are going to do."

Henry Ford
Industrialist

"What was the greatest thing before sliced bread?"

Bill Gates
Chairman
Microsoft Corporation

"A man or a nation is not placed upon this earth to do merely what is pleasant and what is profitable. It is often called upon to carry out what is both unpleasant and unprofitable, but if it is obviously right it is mere shirking not to undertake it."

Conon Doyle
English Author
"The Tragedy of the Korosko"

"Mind you, don't go looking for fights, but if you find yourself in one, make damn sure you win."

Clyde Morrison
To his son, John Wayne
Quoted in Father Knew Best

Attitude

"Self-confidence is the first requisite to great undertakings."

Samuel Johnson
English Critic, Author

"I have learned to use the word impossible with the greatest caution."

Werner von Braun
German Rocket Scientist

"Every day you may make progress. Yet there will stretch out before you an ever-lengthening, ever-ascending, ever-improving path. You know you will never get to the end of the journey. But this, so far from discouraging, only adds to the glory of the climb."

Sir Winston Churchill
British Statesman

Business

"I don't want any yes-men around me. I want everybody to tell me the truth even if it costs them their jobs."

Samuel Goldwyn
Movie Mogul

"Advertising doesn't cost; it pays."

Billboard in Kansas

Courage

"For without belittling the courage with which men have died, we should never forget those acts of courage with which men have lived."

John F. Kennedy
U.S. President

"Courage is rightly esteemed the first of human qualities, because it is the quality which guarantees all others."

Sir Winston Churchill
British Statesman

"Bravery is being the only one who knows you're afraid."

David Hackworth
Soldier, Author

"Conscience is the root of all true courage; if a man would be brave, let him obey his conscience."

James Freeman Clarke
Unitarian Minister
Writer

"Courage is fear hanging on a minute longer."

George S. Patton
General, U.S. Army

<u>Definitions</u>

"Conscience is, in most men, an anticipation of the opinion of others."

Sir Henry Taylor
Governor General, Bahamas

"A professor is one who talks in someone else's sleep."

W. H. Auden
English Poet

"A decision is the action an executive must take when he has information so incomplete that the answer does not suggest itself."

Arthur William Radford
Admiral, U.S. Navy

"A proverb is one man's wit and all men's wisdom."

Bertrand Russell
British Philosopher

"A synonym is a word you use when you can't spell the other one."

Baltasar Gracian
Occupation Unknown

"A pessimist is a man who thinks all women are bad. An optimist is a man who hopes they are."

Chauncey Depew
Politician, Orator

"Egotist: A person of low taste, more interested in himself than in me."

Ambrose Bierce
Author

"Perseverance is the hard work you do after you get tired of doing the hard work you already did."

Newt Gingrich
Politician, Educator

"A cynic is a man who, when he smells flowers, looks around for a coffin."

H. L. Mencken
Satirist, Social Critic

"Committee: A group of men who individually can do nothing but as a group decide that nothing can be done."

Fred Allen
Comedian

"An intellectual is someone who can listen to the William Tell Overture and not think of the Lone Ranger."

Anonymous

Education

"It is the mark of an educated mind to be able to entertain a thought without accepting it."

Aristotle
Greek Philosopher

"Learning is not attained by chance. It must be sought for with ardor and attended to with diligence."

Abigail Adams
Letter to her son, John Quincy Adams

Experience

"Experience is what you get when you didn't get what you wanted."

Italian Saying

"Human beings , who are almost unique in having the ability to learn from the experience of others, are also remarkable for their apparent disinclination to do so."

Douglas Adams
British Author

Great Philosophers

"It is a common failing of mankind never to anticipate the storm when the sea is calm."

Niccolo Machiavelli
Italy

"Eyes are more accurate witnesses than ears."

Heraclitus
Greece

"To see the right and not do it is cowardice."

Confucius
China

Indicision

"In any moment of decision the best thing you can do is the right thing, the next best thing is the wrong thing, and the worst thing you can do is nothing."

Theodore Roosevelt
U.S. President

Insurance

"The devil is in the details."

Unknown

Integrity

"Whoever is careless with the truth in small matters cannot be trusted with the important matters."

Albert Einstein
Theoretical Physicist

Manners

"Rudeness is the weak man's imitation of strength."

Unknown

Marriage

"In olden times sacrifices were made at the altar, a custom which is still continued."

Helen Rowland
Author

"The best example of a housekeeper is a divorced woman."

George Carlin
Comedian
Brain Droppings

"Husbands are like fires. They go out if unattended."

Zsa Zsa Gabor
Actress

"Marriage is the only war in which you sleep with the enemy."

Francois
Duc de La Rochefoucauld

"My wife and I always hold hands. If I let go, she shops."

Unknown

"I have taken my wife many places far and near, but she keeps finding her way back."

Unknown

"Before marriage, a man declares that he would lay down his life to serve you; after marriage, he won't even lay down his newspaper to talk to you."

Helen Rowland
Author

<u>Military</u>

"Every corporal carries a marshal's baton in his knapsack."

Napoleon Bonaparte
Emperor of France

"In no other profession are the penalties for employing untrained personnel so appalling or so irrevocable as in the military."

Douglas MacArthur
General, U.S. Army

"If we know anything, it is that weakness is provocative."

Donald Rumsfeld
U.S. Secretary of Defense

"I feel that retired generals should never miss an opportunity to remain silent concerning matters for which they are no longer responsible."

H. Norman Schwarzkopf
General, U.S. Army

"Fatigue makes cowards of us all."

George S. Patton
General, U.S. Army
War As I Knew It

"Unfortunately, magnanimity is often seen as weakness by those on the receiving end. It's easy to be sensitive, tolerant and multicultural--it's the default mode of the age--yet, when you persist in being sensitive to the insensitive, tolerant of the intolerant, and impeccably multicultural about the avowedly unicultural, don't be surprised if they take it for weakness."

Mark Steyn <u>America Alone</u>
(On the war on terrorism)

Opportunity

"Wherever we look upon this earth, the opportunities take shape within the problems."

Unknown

"The follies which a man regrets most in his life are those which he didn't commit when he had the opportunity."

Helen Rowland
Author

Prayer

Build me a son, O Lord, who will be strong enough to know when he is weak, and brave enough to face himself when he is afraid, one who will be proud and unbending in honest defeat, and humble and gentle in victory."

Douglas MacArthur
General, U.S. Army
"A Father's Prayer"

Presidents/Politicians

"America is great not because of what she has done for herself but because of what she has done for others."

John McCain
U.S. Senator

"The difference between a politician and a statesman is: a politician thinks of the next election and a statesman thinks of the next generation."

James Freeman Clarke
Unitarian Minister, Writer

"People never lie so much as after a hunt, during a war, or before an election."

Otto Von Bismarck
German Statesman

"In a democracy, a man who does not listen, cannot lead."

David Broder
Political Journalist

"We, the people, elect leaders not to rule but to serve."

Dwight D. Eisenhower
U.S. President

"In this business, you have to be prepared to make a few enemies in order to have enough friends."

Unknown

"The opportunist thinks of me and today. The statesman thinks of us and tomorrow."

Dwight D. Eisenhower
U.S. President

"In my many years, I have come to the conclusion that one useless man is a shame, two is a law firm and three or more is a congress."

John Adams
U.S. President

"Many forms of government have been tried, and will be tried in this world of sin and woe. No one pretends that democracy is perfect or all-wise. Indeed, it has been said that democracy is the worst form of government except all those other forms that have been tried from time to time."

Winston Churchill
British Prime Minister

<u>Proverbs</u>

"One of life's greatest mysteries is how the boy who wasn't good enough to marry your daughter can be the father of the smartest grandchild in the world."

Jewish

"One can pay back the loan of gold, but one dies forever in debt to those who are kind."

Malayan

"If you are patient in one moment of anger, you will escape a hundred days of sorrow."

Chinese

"It is better to be a mouse in a cat's mouth than a man in a lawyer's hands."

Spanish

"Fortune favors the bold but abandons the timid."

Latin

Religion

"One person with a belief is equal to a force of 99 who have only interests."

John Stuart Mill
English Philosopher

Retirement/Growing Older

"Wisdom doesn't come automatically with old age. Nothing does--except wrinkles. It's true, some wines improve with age, but only if the grapes were good in the first place."

Abigale Van Buren
Advice Columnist

"The young have aspirations that never come to pass; the old have reminiscences of what never happened."

Saki (AKA Hector Munro)
British Author

"What a wonderful life I've had. I only wish I'd realized it sooner."

Collette Goddard
Actress

"As you grow older, you'll find that the only things you regret are the things you didn't do."

Zachary Scott
Actor

"Old age is not so bad when you consider the alternatives."

Maurice Chevalier
French Actor

"The secret to staying young is to live honestly, eat slowly, and lie about your age."

Lucille Ball
Comedian, Actress

"The older we get, the more clearly we remember the things that never happened."

Unknown

"Don't worry about avoiding temptation. As you grow older, it will avoid you."

Unknown

"We could certainly slow down the aging process if it had to work its way through Congress."

Will Rogers
Humorist, Author

I don't have anything against old people. I hope to be one some day."

Charles Barkley
NBA Player

<u>Risk</u>

"All glory comes from daring to begin."

Anonymous

"To laugh is to risk appearing the fool. To weep is to risk appearing sentimental. To reach out for another is to risk involvement. To express feeling is to risk expressing your true self. To place your ideas, your dreams before the crowd is to risk their loss. To love is to risk being loved in return. To live is to risk dying. To hope is to risk despair. To try is to risk failure. But risks must be taken, because the greatest hazard in life is to risk nothing. The person who risks nothing, does nothing, has nothing, and is nothing. He may avoid suffering and sorrow, but he simply cannot learn, feel, change, love, grow, live. Chained by his certitudes, he is a slave, he has forfeited freedom. Only a person who risks is free."

Unknown

Success/Failure

"What would you attempt to do if you knew you could not fail?"

Unknown

"Remembering that you are going to die is the best way to avoid the fear that you have something to lose."

Steve Jobs
Founder, Apple Computer

"There are no secrets to success. Don't waste time looking for them. Success is the result of perfection, hard work, learning from failure, loyalty to those for whom you work, and persistence."

Colin Powell
General, U.S. Army
U.S. Secretary of State

"The difference between a successful person and others is not the lack of strength, not the lack of knowledge, but rather in a lack of will."

Vince Lombardi
Football Coach
Green Bay Packers

__Wealth__

"There is a great deal of difference between earning a great deal of money and being rich."

Marlene Dietrich
German Actress

__Work__

Most people work just hard enough not to get fired and get paid just enough money not to quit."

George Carlin
Comedian
<u>Brain Droppings</u>

"A fine quotation

is a diamond

on the finger of a man of wit,

but a pebble

in the hand of a fool."

Joseph Roux

About the Author

Bob Moscatelli received his undergraduate degree from the United States Military Academy at West Point, New York. He spent 26 years on active duty as an Army officer retiring as a colonel in 1984.

He holds a masters degree in public administration from Shippensburg State University in Shippensburg, Pennsylvania. He is also a graduate of the United States Army War College in Carlisle, Pennsylvania.

After retiring from the Army in 1984, Bob worked as a financial programmer for eight years in Colorado Springs, Colorado. He and his wife, Bonnie, now live in Frisco, Colorado, where Bob is a former mayor.

Printed in the United States
101965LV00001B/172/A